TAJ MAHAL

POETIC VERSES THAT CELEBRATE LOVE

DR. NEHA PALIWAL SHARMA

Copyright © Dr. Neha Paliwal Sharma
All Rights Reserved.

To

All who love & care from heart!

Contents

1. Eternal Love: I am...the Taj Mahal!

A classic, chaste, unblemished marathon of compassion
A witness to eternal love and countless epics …yes it's me,
Live evidence of ever alluring God-like devotion
I have seen it all… remarkable yet elusive to brightest of thee,
I am…the Taj Mahal!
The grand retrospection of an artist's imagination
The Golden chapter of world history…is embedded on my aged
chest,
Dousing the inferno of hatred & evil conflagration
The abode to Shah & Mumtaz…I am the sepulcher where they
calmly rest,
I am…the Taj Mahal!
Radiating with deep-rooted charm…ever glowing bright
The monument of love…world's most treasured sparkling jewel,
Draped all over in milky white shafts on moon-lit nights
Lofty minarets merging into heavens …I am where the divinity
dwells,
I am…the Taj Mahal!
Irrefutable icon of untainted ardor …that was larger than life

For historians, sages & aficionados… a place of worship &
adulation,
Rendezvous of assorted cultures and mores that mesmerize
Soothing all hearts with my charismatic charm…exquisite
global constellation,
I am…the Taj Mahal!
Quenching the insatiable thirst …an yearning for tranquility &
affection
Timeless muse for painters & versifiers…secret of concord I
unfold,
Maintenance I tell you my folks…is much arduous than creation
Take care of this antique gem of yours…that thou all fondly
adore,
I am…the Taj Mahal!

2. Bhagwad Gita – The Song of GOD's Love!

The melodious essence of divinity
Sung by none other than YOU…O KRISHNA, My Lord!
Torch-bearer for your disciples that you are
Hence gave discourse…to eliminate spiritual discord!
A warehouse of sacred knowledge
For harmony in our daily lives,
The science of realizing the self
Art of extracting honey…from the blissful bee-hive!
At the launch of mêlée between the good and evil
In the battle- field of heavenly Kuruksetra,
When Arjuna faced the moral dilemma to fight his own…
YOU rescued him…with YOUR holy grace!
"The ultimate truth"…YOU said 'O Partha,
Is not what your two eyes see here,
All is a mirage; except ME…look out
I am universal…found every-where!"
"Birth and Death…Joy and Sorrow
Are nothing…but like changing seasons,
An enlightened soul …worthy of liberation
Is not perturbed by such transitions!"

"How can you slain or cause to kill
The indestructible soul…all pervasive,
Don't hesitate in discharging your duties
As it would be a sin…to stand passive!"
"Just do what is befitting you
Do not care for the fruits…thus borne,
Strive for yoga…the art of all work
Transcend above…the materialistic thorns!"
"Let desires flow through you…like an ocean
Ever overflowing with rivers…but always still,
Let the 'axe of detachment' cut threads of lust, anger & greed
Awaken yourself with a sturdy will!"
"Just surrender unto me…the universal power
Surpassing all forms of religious convictions,
You will come to me…without fail…do trust
Unscathed from all sinful reactions!"
To enlighten wanderers of dark worldly lanes
The supreme eternal secret …YOU disclosed,
Through the sermon to YOUR great warrior friend
YOU opened the divine doors…that were so far closed!
What can frighten the one …Who's Charioteer YOU are?
A soul surrendered unto you…Can ride through all worldly
paddy fields,
You are all…source of all…advent and end of all
Its YOUR heavenly adobe…where all are meant to yield!

3. Earthquake: Love for Mankind!

Many-a-lives have been transformed into wreck
The bleeding, the wounded, rising toll of the dead,
'Divine Vengeance' or label it 'Fury' of nature
Nothing I see…except agony wide-spread!
Worst hit are thousands of innocent souls
The infants, the brood, none have been spared,
In flick of second…scores of generations wiped out
Leaving behind grieving fathers and,
Miserable mothers who howl!
Searching for signs of life … digging up the debris
"Was it a school or was it a home?",
"Was it a temple or shrine or a mosque?"
All eyes are moist & all heads cast down,
No man can make out from this 'muddy tomb'!
Commotion, turmoil, dual between 'soil' & human race
It's an upshot for that we did to flora and fauna,
Our slayer being none other than the very giver of grains
The quake, the tremors, 'live coverage of pain',
Mockery of emotions…or sharing the mayhem!
Ah…we are the victims

But who do we blame and accuse,
To escape this anguish…none has any excuse
Time shall heal the terrible wounds that we bear,
Life has to move on…a beam of hope still there!

4. Hero: A Soldier's Love for Motherland!

Laying down his life ...so that we may live
Our real hero...he is the knight in shining armor,
Fought face to face with the intruders
Shielded thousands from the demon of terror!
Though we may feel indebted to him...but
Numeral tears in our eyes...can't equate a jot of his blood,
While many ducked ... took cover to be safe
He guarded all...like a solid-rock shade!
Preferred to be shot in chest...than showing back
Confronting fear of losing the loved ones,
This sacrifice & valor will always be unmatched
Salutation to all mothers...who yield such sons!
Making way through mortar & gun-powder...
Didn't blink an eye...when asked to fight,
No threat, no snag could deter his passion
He risked his all...to give us freedom from strife!
Hey feisty savior, Hey liberator
O Warrior the great... hats off to you,
Such indomitable zeal & high-spirit
Where else could we find...if not in thou?

TAJ MAHAL

Doing full justice to the medals & garb you don
Engaging in battles with coldhearted slayers,
A contrast to perpetrators of heinous crimes
We deem …you are the way GOD answers prayers !

5. Time Flies: A Saga of Mother's Love!

Time flies…no wings though it has
But this stallion rushes at the light's pace!
It was just yesterday
He was lying in her lap,
Free from all the whim-whams
Feeling Mother's care, love & caress!
Years pass by; "Boy" grows into "Man"
Didn't feel like hug her wrinkled face!
A liberated bird, soaring to touch the sky
Celebrated with pals, 'loved' all girl-friends,
Handled business matters
With a thorough Gentleman's grace!
Got a wife, was blessed with kids
Who abandoned him…to get ahead in life's race!
At long last…he remembered that selfless, noble soul
But time had flown…. Impatient voyager it is,
"Mother" figure was now synonymous to ashes
His dreams to finally serve her…were set ablaze!
"Oh Mother…mother! You left me mid-way" he mourns
"Here I stand next to your grave, waiting for thy gentle touch"

"All life you covered me up in your warmth
And I discarded thou…to turn you into ash!"
Guilty he stood…While silent she lay
Such unadulterated love…how could he abase?
"A vessel with no harbor , A life with no aim
What have I become? Mere pawn of fate's game"
"Hey Mother…come back
And soothe my pain…,
Cuddle me up once more
With your Godly embrace!"
But she would not listen…a "Cruel Master" time is
Mother is now calm, while the lonely son wails!
Learns the lesson of his life
But it's now too late,
Time has flown…
The deep loss now won't abate!

6. It's you: Love of a Father!

An Epitome of adoration
Unwary, Soft …and ever loving,
It's you O Father…
Who is sans parallel!
A ray of hope…in most hazy days
Unscathed from sins & forgiving,
It's you O Father…
Who is sans parallel!
A spark of joy…in many ways
Unstrained in times most trying,
It's you O Father…
Who is sans parallel!
A pious deity in human form
Untouched from worldly stroking,
It's you O Father…
Who is sans parallel!
A mystical figure…a known personage
Uncolored yet hues of ardor radiating,
It's you O Father…
Who is sans parallel!

TAJ MAHAL

A blessing of an elderly
Unfound, miracles & luck showering,
It's you O Father…
Who is sans parallel!
A reason to bring smile
Unchanged, inert yet eternally moving,
It's you O Father…
Who is sans parallel!
A child's ignorant innocence
Untainted, warm and touching,
It's you O Father…
Who is sans parallel!
A blooming flower in emerald garden
Unpicked, colorful and stimulating,
It's you O Father…
Who is sans parallel!
A glimpse of the invincible
Unseen, supreme, awakening,
It's you O Father…
Who is sans parallel!

7. When I die…O My Child!

When I die…O My Child
I wish I must die…for a noble cause,
And serve my life for others because
I think life is merely a circus,
Where each one of us is a comic
For others' purpose!
On my death, do not lament
Nor you be sad and upset,
For even after I collapse
My sun will still not set!
When I die…
You would feel my tender in the
Golden streaks of sun,
And my love's warmth in the sunrays
Will lift up your spirits & make thou feel gay!
When I die…
You would feel me blossom in the
Fragrance of your garden roses,
Where my charming aroma will satiate thy noses!
My soft scent will appear to thou

TAJ MAHAL

A fondant,
So don't fragile your happiness
And do not feel the pain!
When I die…
You would hear my voice, when break on the rocks,
The impish tides of the sea
And hear me,
In the humming birds, the buzzing bees, the blowing breeze
And also in a horse's whinny!
When I die…
You would feel my hand's touch,
In the monsoon showers that'll soothe your scorched fore-heads
When drift above you, the thundering
Lightning rainy Hyades!
When I die…
Don't shed pearl-like tears thou,
For even after my demise
I shall remain near you!
When I die…
And terminates my breath,
Please do not consider me dead
Even though I may lie in the lap of the thorny mortality
Life itself is not a rose's bed!
When I die…
You'll not perceive sound of my heart-beats,
Nor would feel any pulse in me
My cold palm's touch will not please you

But …
My triumphed face will make thee glee!
Don't let this parting drive you frantic
Rather, fare me well with a smile,
Pay heed O my innocent child
To my all of this mantic!
Life is but a dream…& death steals it all
Ergo, I tell you…for my reason,
Do not let yourself ever fall!
Ah! This very death, a blessing or a curse
While it could make you feel the pain,
I might be gone…but yet be there
For…my part in you will still remain!

8. Unborn: An Irony of Love!

Slaughter of innocence…in the womb
Massacre…hushing faint cries of child unborn,
What's her fault…that you punish her for?
She too has a right to live…a right to carry on!
She is the root…from which all originates
The underpinning…human race foundation,
One who gives birth…bears this carnage brunt
Soaked in blood-bath…slumber on bed of thorn!
She could have been a crutch for ailing father
Like her brother…if given a chance to be full-grown,
Could have wiped out tears from mother's eyes
Only if…you hadn't dug out that social key-stone!
How impassive & hollow have all become?
Volte-face fiends…saintly attires all adorn,
Gift to bear…woman's ornament or binding shackles
The one who yields…deprived of privilege to be born!
Conflict underneath…tender desires ruthlessly set ablaze
Mother forced to part with own flesh…in the name of tradition,
Ashen faces, cold hearts and blind-folded are all eyes
Mute spectators…bear testimony to a future torn!

What's the mistake…that she's made to pay for?
Why no heart melts on hearing her moan?
Doing the dreadful wrong…in the guise of just
How come supreme authority's tiara have we worn?
A child is a child…not a boy…or a girl
GOD made them equal…without any mean classification,
Let's make a pledge…to abolish this infanticide curse before it's late
Shaken sources…jointly…need to be fairly re-build upon!

9. Love Yourself…Rediscover Self!

Long, Unwinding Road……That Life Is
Walk down the lane undeterred ,
GOD certainly has a plan for thou
Discover it….and Rediscover self!
When the dream-mirror falls upon
Broken pieces you see… everywhere scattered,
Gather the strength that's hidden in thou
Discover it…and Rediscover self!
Break all the chains that are binding you
What's the point….living shattered?
Start afresh…it's a Brand New Day
Discover it…and Rediscover self!
Adversity tells thou friends n foes
Some stand by…some leave you hammered,
A gauge tool it is in disguise
Discover it…and Rediscover self!
Spring follows autumn year after year
Let go of the arid leaves gathered,
Lush pasture waiting with open arms
Discover it…and Rediscover self!

Love is all that matters...